Bowls Rules OK

Chris Mills

Good Bowling

Chris Mills

'Today's Bowler'

A & C Black · London

To Violet

First published 1994 by
A & C Black (Publishers) Ltd
35 Bedford Row, London WC1R 4JH

Text © 1994 Chris Mills
Laws © English Bowling Association

ISBN 0 7136 3833 8

A CIP catalogue record for this book
is available from the British Library.

Acknowledgement
Illustrations by Barry Gurbutt.

Phototypeset in 10½/11pt Souvenir Light by
Rowland Phototypesetting Ltd,
Bury St Edmunds, Suffolk
Printed and bound in Great Britain by
Redwood Books, Trowbridge, Wiltshire

●●

Contents

●●

Bowls sizes

Size in inches	Size Number	May be rounded off Metric (mm)
4–9/16	00	116
4–5/8	0	117
4–3/4	1	121
4–13/16	2	122
4–7/8	3	124
4–15/16	4	125
5	5	127
5–1/16	6	129
5–1/8	7	131

Introduction

He was playing at Plymouth a rubber of bowls
When the great Armada came;
But he said, 'They must wait their turn, good souls,'
And then stooped, and finished his game.

It is, perhaps, appropriate to begin any book on bowls with lines dedicated to that great event of 1588, when Sir Francis Drake became one of England's legendary heroes by defeating the Spanish Armada. Not only that: by doing so in that particular manner he showed the English to be a nation of sportsmen and women who could put their sport above all else. Drake's exploits at Plymouth Hoe also gave future schoolchildren their first introduction to the game of bowls.

To all participants, whether or not they play under Association, Federation or Crown Green rules, bowls is the greatest game in the world. No other game, it has been written, is so provocative of genial mirth, nor more conducive to good fellowship. And, by all accounts, it's a simple game too!

All you have to do is roll a spherical object of around 3½lb in weight (a 'bowl') at a smaller, stationary white ball (the 'jack') as near as you can get it, even touching it. Now what could be simpler than that?

A Canadian handbook in 1902 stated that: 'Bowls is a quiet and philosophic amusement which depends for its success on a thorough realisation that nothing happens in it, any more than real life, exactly according to scientific calculation.' While this may be true in some cases, if anything has changed in the game since the early part of the century it is its competitiveness.

As children we all learn to play games through the laws by which they are controlled. Later, as adults, when either continuing in a sport or taking up a new one, those laws are still an important factor in our success or otherwise. In many cases a lack of knowledge of the laws that govern a game can be obvious during play. Bowls, in particular, seems to have its fair share of those who, while knowing all the basics and the mechanics of the game, seem sadly lacking in knowledge when a dispute arises over the laws.

Throughout my own bowling career, I have been amazed at the number of bowlers who are not fully aware of the laws that govern the game they play. I have found that this particularly applies to those who have taken up the game merely for pleasure, the 'non-competitive' or 'social' players. Since it's not their intention to take the game too seriously, obviously they feel it is unnecessary to bother with more than an outline of the rules governing it.

This was more the case when bowls was considered by most as a sport for the elderly. Now that it can be seen readily as a sport for all ages, I hope that knowledge of the laws will improve, since players are now more keen to establish their skills at club, county and national level.

Note   Throughout the book bowls players are referred to individually as 'he'. This should, of course, be taken to mean 'he or she' where appropriate.

Mitchell's laws

The modern laws of flat green, or 'level green', bowls were framed by a Glasgow solicitor and keen bowler, William W Mitchell. (However, prior to that laws had been drawn up by King Charles II, James the Duke of York, and the Duke of Buckingham in 1670.) In 1848 Mitchell attended a meeting at the Glasgow Town Hall, convened to consider a proposition to form a national association. No decision to form an association was taken at that meeting or, in fact, at a further meeting the following year, but members expressed a desire for the drafting of a code of laws.

Single-handedly, Mitchell set about drafting a set of laws. These laws were subsequently adopted in 1893, with some modifications, and issued as the Laws of the Game by the Scottish Bowling Association. Later still, in 1905, when the International Bowling Board (now the World Bowls Board) was formed, it adopted the Scottish Bowling Association laws. The laws of the flat green game throughout the world are substantially founded on those drafted out by Mitchell in 1849.

In 1865, Mitchell published *A Manual of Bowl-Playing* which incorporated his laws and, among other things, gave instructions to skips on how they could make visual signs to colleagues informing them of the team's present position, without revealing their tactics to the opposing skip. His instruction of throwing out the arm horizontally, followed by a wave of the hand and arm, to indicate the degree of strength that should be applied to the bowl, is still used today to signal to a player that his team is shots down and he must *be up!* It really requires few, if any, words.

Club officials and coaches should do more to develop the attitude, particularly among beginners, that a sound knowledge of the laws is as an essential part of the player's equipment as his bowls. One of the most successful columns in *Bowls International* magazine is the 'Umpire's Corner', which is fronted by the secretary of the English Bowls Umpires Association, Norman Deeprose. It is obvious from the many questions that flood in to the magazine that a great deal of confusion abounds regarding the laws, even among those who should know better.

The Laws of the Game, by their very nature, are transmitted in terms that are not always fully understandable. Like most legal documents (and the laws were, after all, written originally by a solicitor), they seek to cover every possible aspect and eventuality, although in doing so some ambiguities are unwittingly thrown up.

The first 'law' is, in fact, a series of definitions which are designed to make the laws that follow easier to understand. We'll take a quick run through these definitions before starting the first chapter.

Definitions

Controlling body – the body or authority having immediate control of the conditions under which a match is played. The pecking order is: the World Bowls Board, the national bowling authority, the state, division or county association, and finally the club that owns the green on which the match is played.

Skip – the player who's in charge of the team and the last line of attack or defence. The **team** means either a fours, triples or pair, whereas a **side** means any agreed number of teams, whose combined scores determine the results of the match. A **four** means a team of four players, with positions in order of playing of lead, second, third and skip.

Master bowl – a bowl can be described technically as a biased spheroid with rings marked on either side. The important point to remember is that the smaller rings are always on the inside of the bowl when delivered. The 'master' bowl, however, is in a class of its own, being a bowl approved by the World Bowls Board (WBB) as having the minimum bias required as well as complying in all respects with the Laws of the Game. A bowl of the same bias as the master bowl is kept in 'custody' by each national association, and is provided for use by each officially licensed tester. Just for the record, a 'set' of bowls means four bowls all of a matched set which are of the same manufacture and the same size, weight, colour, bias and, where applicable, serial number and engraving.

(With this in mind, you must be wondering why so many bowls act so differently, but that's when you discover that the word 'minimum' is crucial.)

Bowl (in course) – the path that a bowl takes after it leaves your hand, whether it is as you intended or not, is described for the purpose of the laws as being on its 'course'. It's often a curse, but from the moment it leaves your hand to when it finally comes to rest, is its 'course'. This will become important later when you learn about such intricacies as the 'speed of the green' and 'touchers'.

Bowl (jack high) – besides giving its name to television programmes and a number of local newspaper bowls writers, this term also means that a bowl is level with the jack. It can be a useful guide to players, and provides for one of the best known hand signals in the game.

Bowl or jack (displaced) – bowls may stay in one place while you are playing, or they may move about. Sometimes they move legitimately, or they may be moved by 'outside forces' not sanctioned by the laws. Feeding birds or lazy dogs could be categorised as 'outside agencies'!

Head – it must be a little confusing to the beginner to be asked to put one in the head! It means the form or position that the bowls and jack take, within the boundaries of the rink, as they are played throughout a particular end. As you will know, or will quickly find out, the head can change rapidly as the end progresses.

Mat (line) – for the purposes of the law and to assist with all measurements, this means the edge which is used for delivery, nearest to the front ditch. When measurements are taken they should always be from the centre of the mat, which is of a defined size.

Pace of the green – in itself it sounds simple. It is the number of seconds from when a bowl leaves the bowler's hand to when it comes to rest on a jack placed 30 yards away. When you start to work out the reasons why a 'fast' green is anything from 16 seconds upwards, and a 'slow' green around 12 seconds and below, then it becomes confusing!

There are many other terms that are used in bowls, many of which are a part of bowls' own folklore. You'll find a chapter on these starting on page 35.

Important note

This book is not intended as a substitute for a thorough study of the Laws of the Game issued by the WBB. But hopefully, it will cut through the jargon with a more down to earth approach that should make a knowledge of the game a great deal clearer. All the laws referred to are printed at the end of the book with the courtesy of the EBA.

The green and equipment

Flat green bowls is played outdoors on a level surface which is usually grass, although it can be of an artificial nature. Indoors the game is played on carpets made of felt or other synthetic materials. In theory, nothing could be simpler than the size and shape of a bowling green. It should form a square (of not less than 120 feet nor more than 132 feet), be level, and be provided with boundaries in the form of a ditch and a bank. A square lawn with its own dry moat!

However, we all know that greens come in a wider variety of shapes and sizes than the definition simply suggests. The indoor laws differ in the respect that a green is referred to in terms of a single rink of set proportions, and is made up of one or more of these up to an undefined number, whereas an outdoor green nearly always means a square of six rinks, which can be bowled over in different directions (i.e. north to south; east to west). Indoor bowling, however, only takes place north to south or east to west (depending on how the building is constructed!), and always across the seams of the carpet lengths that make up the full surface. Therefore, the green doesn't need to be a square. It also means that in the case of the indoor green, while it may have ditches and banks on four sides, only the two ends need to conform to the correct standards.

The birth of the eight-rinker in the 1970s at Teeside heralded a new era in indoor bowls, although the majority of stadia are still of the conventional six rinks. (Old habits die hard!)

SPIRIT LEVEL

In the early days, outdoor bowling took place on any flat area of grass. The level square of sward that constituted an outdoor green gradually evolved with ditches and banks throughout the twentieth century as boundaries and shapes became far more defined. In some cases it was quite easy to make the various conversions; in others it was found that the closeness of certain obstacles posed problems, and boundary lines had to be adjusted within given parameters.

As you can see, bowls greens can vary considerably in size, less in shape, and many bowlers will testify that finding a 'level' green can be quite difficult. New bowlers will quickly learn that greens are usually criticised more by those who have lost than by winners!

Each surface, whether it is grass or synthetic, has its own peculiarities in terms of resistance, consistency and surroundings. But one of the biggest differences between

indoor and outdoor greens is their maintenance. Outdoor greens require a lot of time, patience and hard work involving a variety of expensive pieces of equipment. With indoor greens, it's just a case of employing a large vacuum!

There is usually a marker on the bank to indicate the centre of the rink, and also a marker on the two sides of the rink at each end. Until 1993 it was mandatory to have the rinks on an outdoor green ruled off by 'strings' drawn tightly over the surface to form a boundary, but this never applied indoors and much lobbying by those who saw little point in this exercise saw to the termination of the practice outdoors as well.

Remember: a 'green' is the whole playing area, while a 'rink' is both part of it and a group of four (or three in Federation circles) that comprises a team.

The bowls

A bowl, the tool-in-trade of any bowler, has been described as: *a device created with extraordinary scientific precision, never to go in the direction required with the object of torturing the person playing with it.*

As in most sports – while the batsman has his favourite bat, the snooker player his cue, and the tennis player his racket – bowlers have their *own* bowls and rarely discard them because they are virtually indestructible. In the very early days, bowls were made of a variety of materials, including metal, stone and bone. In fact, it is suspected that the heads of opponents killed in battle were used by some bloodthirsty bowlers in times gone by.

As the game progressed through the centuries, it became more and more popular to play with wooden bowls. First they were made with a variety of timbers, from apple wood to box wood, but then they began to be shaped from lignum vitae, a particularly hard wood from the West Indies and one of only a handful of types of wood that sinks in water. No one knows exactly when lignum vitae started to be used for bowls manufacture, but the island of San Domingo, where most of the timber comes from, was discovered by Christopher Columbus in 1492 and introduced into Europe in 1508 by the Spaniards. Rumour has it that ships' carpenters constructed bowls out of lignum vitae for Sir Francis Drake while they waited in Plymouth to set sail on his round-the-world voyages. At one time, the wood was also used to make ships' ball-bearings.

There are many myths and legends surrounding how bowls developed from being merely round lumps of wood to today's sophisticated, composition tools-of-the-trade, with their tantalising tricks. This is the reason why bowls are still referred to as 'woods', particularly by the older generation who still remember their first set of 'trundlers'.

Although larger, lignums could still be lighter, volume for volume, than composition bowls of a similar size, an important factor when the 'weight-for-size' rule applied. When this was universally scrapped in 1980 for the rule that merely stipulated the maximum and minimum size and weight for bowls without attempting to relate one to the other, it completely changed the composition of bowls. It allowed for smaller sizes to be fabricated from a denser material, giving the same advantage to those with smaller hands by allowing for heavyweight versions of the smaller sizes, although the larger sizes could also be produced as both medium and heavyweight.

Today, virtually all bowls used in the flat green game are made from plastic, although the laws do allow them to be made also of rubber, and they can be black or brown in colour. They are made in identical sets of four to extremely fine tolerances, the majority from a phenolic-resin powder. The minimum amount of bias is strictly regulated by the sport's governing bodies, whose 'official' stamp must be carried on each bowl and may need to be checked after specific periods. Bowls come in nine sizes, from 00 to 7, with the maximum weight being 3½lbs, while the maximum diameter is 5½ inches (composition) or 5¼ inches (lignum vitae). The bias effect of the bowl is created in the moulding by one side being slightly flattened, leaving the other side heavier. Thus as the bowl rolls up the green, it will experience two forces: the first is the forward force caused by the propulsion from the hand; the other is the sideways force exercised by the extra weight on one side. Therefore, a bowl doesn't run in a straight line for all of its course, but takes a curved path as it slows down. The faster a bowl is moving, the more the forward thrust takes effect. When it slows down the sideways force becomes stronger, pulling the bowl inwards.

The conditions of a green play a large part in the running of a bowl, whether it is outdoors on grass or, to a lesser degree, on indoor carpets. A close-cut, hard green on a sunny day will offer far less resistance to a bowl than one that has thick grass on a damp day.

Most bowlers would agree that it is the bias of the bowl that makes the game as fascinating as it is. This is where one peculiar anomaly in terminology comes into the game. On a sun-baked green a bowl will take longer to reach its objective than on a green that is soft, wet and grassy. The reason for this is quite simple. If the green is

'fast' then a bowl will take a wider line (arc) to reach its target and will therefore take longer than on a 'slow' green, where the line to the jack is narrower and so the bowl arrives more quickly.

The life span of the official stamp carried on bowls is ten years, expiring on December 31 of the year carried on the imprint. Bowls is said to be a friendly game played in a true sporting spirit, but if you suspect that your opponent is taking advantage by not playing with a 'legal' set of bowls, there are specific laws that deal with an objection.

Object immediately after a match to the correct authority, and pay a fee (refundable if the objection is upheld) for the privilege. It doesn't happen that often – indeed, I can think of only a couple of cases in the last ten years. But I do remember once pointing out to a very well-known player that his bowls stamp was 'out-of-date'. It pays to check your equipment on occasions!

Mats and jacks

The way in which it is dropped on the green and tossed about when not in use, may give you the impression that the mat is an unwanted part of bowls equipment. But, technically, the game can't be played without it. In the early days, when the quality of the greens in use was not quite so crucial, a piece of wood known as a 'trig' was used, and in nineteenth century Scotland a 'cloth' became the regulation mat.

To comply with today's laws, the mat must be rectangular. It is usually made of rubber, and it should measure 24 × 14 inches. Most mats have a 2-inch white border and black centre, although this is not mandatory. Despite the laws, you will still see a few car mats used as substitutes, and I'm sure a few prayers get said when bowlers are 'on the mat'.

The jack, meanwhile, fully expects to get knocked about. When round stones were cast as bowls, the target was usually a cone or some free-standing object. It is suspected that the change from 'cone' to 'ball' came around the fourteenth century, and that the term 'jack' is from the Latin word *jactus* meaning a 'cast' or 'throw'. Whatever the origin, it is a known fact that the round ball we know today has been around in some material or other for at least four centuries. In the early part of this century it was made of porcelain but is now made of phenolic resin (outdoors) and heavy-density aluminium (indoors). (In crown green bowls the jack is like a miniature bowl, and is similarly biased.) In most cases a flat green jack is white, although yellow jacks are becoming more and more popular indoors because they are certainly easier to see under artificial lighting. Jacks must conform to specific diameters (not less than $2^{15}/_{32}$ inches or more than $2^{17}/_{32}$ inches indoors). Outdoor jacks weigh between 8 and 10 ounces; indoor jacks are heavier, weighing between $13\frac{1}{2}$ and 16 ounces.

Clothing and shoes

Battered and worn, bandless and torn,
  Any old hat will do.
Out-of-fashion and crushed, always unbrushed,
  But never by any chance new.

The rest of the sporting world may have gone to ruin, with
tennis players now appearing in shirts, shorts and skirts
that owe a great deal to the whims of the design world,
and cricketers wearing clothing that looks more like
pyjamas, but apart from the coloured tops worn by
competitors in the World Indoor Championships and
other international and televised events, bowls has
remained fairly rigid in its dress code.

Clothing codes vary depending on the club's location
and its application of domestic rules. It used to be the rule
that south of the Watford Gap bowlers appeared on the
green in all white clothing, while in the north of the
country more or less anything went. The general rule
seems to be that at county and national level bowlers play
in all white, while it is 'white above the waist and greys
below' for most club games, with 'whites' in special
matches. Add to this ties and blazers for the men, and
special waistcoats and skirts for the women. Check the

team-sheet to see what clothing you should wear in the match that you have been chosen to play in. Assume nothing – always check!

Outdoor games are subject to weather conditions and games can often be interrupted by rain, so you'll need some waterproof clothing, which usually should be all white.

There are no specific rules for hats, with the exception of women of course. The male bowler wears a variety of headgear, one part of his attire that is often strong on eccentricity.

In the case of footwear, the rules are simple but strict. To play you must wear smooth-soled, heel-less footwear at all times on the green! Remember not to put this on until you reach the changing rooms. It's no good having your bowling shoes on in the car, then walking across the car park and picking up all manner of debris on the way.

All this equipment requires something fairly strong in which to carry it. There is a variety of bowls bags on the market that are strong, durable and distinctive.

So that's it. Your game can begin.

Remember: The instrument of all our torture is a 'bowl' not a 'wood'. (After all, people used to play football with a pig's bladder, but playing a game of 'pig's bladder' doesn't quite sound right!) The 'jack' can be termed either a 'cot' or a 'kitty' and, like your bowls, a good deal more sometimes if it doesn't behave! Bowls come in nine sizes (00–7), and indoor jacks (382–434 grams) are heavier than outdoor ones (227–283 grams).

Arranging a game

So what constitutes a game of bowls? Well, bowls is very much what you want to make it, although there are arrangements laid down regarding the number of 'ends' or 'shots' that constitute a 'game'. But if two or more people merely turn up at a green with their bowls and shoes, simply choose sides, then go out on the green and roll merrily away, that's a game – the traditional 'roll-up' which occurs on many an afternoon outdoors during the summer months, although not so much indoors where the sessions tend to be more regimented.

The game itself can take place in a variety of forms ranging from two people playing against each other ('singles'), two per side ('pairs'), three per side ('triples') to four per side ('fours'), or you may simply decide to go out on a green and play on your own.

When there, what do you play? The game can be a specified number of ends (i.e. 18 ends in triples, 21 ends in pairs and fours, or the first to reach 21 shots in singles) or it can be played to a fixed time (i.e. a two-hour session).

Whatever the type or length of game decided, players will play to alternate ends. Bowlers will play first one way 'up' the green, and then back again. There are extenuating circumstances (i.e. a 'dead end') when you may return to the same end, but this will be explained later. However, just think what a drag it would be if you only bowled one way. Imagine having to cart the bowls back up the green to start again. No, much more sensible to play them back and keep the game flowing!

When having a 'roll-up', the tendency is to take whatever rink is available unless you have it all booked up beforehand. Get there first and get the pick of the rinks.

Every club green has its favoured rinks, usually in the middle of the green, and many players prefer certain rinks to others. This choice is often more down to psychology than the physical properties of the rink, but then there is no convincing some players that the green is only as good as the bowler on it!

If playing a league match, the usual form is to tell the opposition what rinks are available (depending on how many rinks are going to be used, i.e. if it was four rinks of fours or three rinks of triples), and the opposing captain will mark the back of the card while choosing who plays who in the same method. That way seems always the fairest because then nobody knows who they are playing or on what rink until they are chosen.

One rule that does apply in the case of competitions is that of the home player nominating which rink he is going to meet his opponent(s) on. There must be no practising on that rink on the day of the competition. (This applies to flat green but not to the crown green code, where players in a competition are often allowed on to the green for an hour's practice before the competition starts.)

As stated earlier, games can be organised for singles play, pairs, triples or fours, and either as one game or a series of games in which the results from each match will go towards the final score of the game as a whole. Those games may operate under a points system which may take into account individual rink scores and the overall match score (i.e. two points for each winning rink and 'x' points for the match score; draws to count half of the total points score). Complicated isn't it!

One interesting variation from the normal game is 'Australian pairs'. In this case, unlike in the UK where the leads play their bowls alternately – the leads first, then the skips – the leads play two bowls alternately, change over with the skips who then play two, and then the leads return to the mat to complete their four bowls, followed by the skips once more.

Add to this the different rules applied by the English Bowling Federation (discussed later), a variety of 'bowls drives', American tournaments, and other such variations, and you will soon realise that bowls – that simple game – is not so easy to work out after all. The laws of bowls have changed little since Charles II drew up his set over 300 years ago. One thing is for certain, his final rule still applies as much to today's bowler as it did to his seventeenth-century predecessor: *Keep your temper! And remember, he who plays at bowls must take the Rubbers.*

Starting the game

In line with many sports, a game of bowls usually starts with the ritualistic handshake followed by the cordial introductions of the players in each team. This sets the pattern for the spirit in which the game is played, while doing nothing to diminish the competitive edge. Etiquette and courtesy have always been a part of the unwritten laws of bowls that mix happily with the specific laws governing the game.

The majority of matches, with the exception of indoor domestic leagues, will start with 'trial ends', which give the players a chance to take a look at the conditions and the run of the rink that they are to be playing on. The laws allow for two trial ends, or an 'up-and-a-downer' as they are often referred to. That is, of course, what the laws allow. If you choose by mutual agreement to alter the conditions by, say, in a triples match just bowling two bowls each way rather than all three, that's up to you. It has become a trend in 'friendly' matches to allow for one shot on the first two ends and dispensing with the trial ends. Get to know your entitlements, and take it from there.

Most games are begun by tossing a coin to open play, the laws then giving the winner of that toss the choice of two options. The first is to take the jack and therefore play first; the second is to pass first play on to the opponent. The toss having been settled, the player to go first will then place the mat and cast the jack. When the jack has been cast correctly, the side going first will also play the first bowl.

It's surprising how many things can go wrong with this simple task. There are several laws that cover mat placing, jack casting and what happens at 'dead ends' or in the event of teams having tied scores at the completion of the required number of ends. Sometimes a draw matters; sometimes it doesn't!

Placing the mat

At the beginning of the opening end the player going first must place the mat lengthwise on the centre of the rink with its front edge exactly 6 feet from the back edge of the green. On subsequent ends the player placing the mat – that is the winner of the previously played end – may choose to place it at any distance from the back edge of the green, providing that the distance from the front edge of the mat to the jack is no less than 70 feet (indoors 75 feet) and the jack is at least 6 feet from the front edge of the green.

The longest play will be with the front edge of the mat 6 feet from the back edge of the green, and the jack 6 feet from the front edge of the green.

Whatever happens, the mat must stay in that position throughout that end.

What if the mat gets inadvertently moved? It can easily happen when a player moves quickly on the mat. The mat should always be straight, so if it gets out of line it must simply be straightened. If it actually moves, it must be placed back as nearly as possible in its original position.

Don't forget, after an end has been completed remove the mat and place it on the bank ready for the next end at that position.

Casting the jack

There is nothing in the laws that actually states when an end starts, although the indoor authorities define an end as meaning the placing of the mat, delivering the jack and all bowls in the same direction, and the determination of the result. But does it begin with the placing of the mat, the casting of the jack or when the first bowl is played? Whatever view you take, the fact is that no start can be made until the jack is cast.

The jack, which is a round ball without bias (on the flat at least, although in crown it's another matter!), should therefore roll in a straight line. However, wherever the jack finishes rolling its position is checked with the centre of the rink. If it is not in line it is moved to the centre line, which will be indicated to the player on the mat by the number-plate in the centre of the rink.

If the jack travels less than 70 feet (75 feet indoors or Federation), goes out of the rink or into the ditch, or a player commits a foot-faulting offence (very rarely picked up), it is then redelivered by an opposing player. (If it is a singles match this will be the other player; if a team game it will be the opposing lead.) The opposing player may also reposition the mat if so desired. Should that player then make a mess of things, it reverts back to the first player.

In years gone by this could technically go on indefinitely until someone got it right, but now the position has changed. If after four attempts (two per side) the jack has still not been delivered correctly, it is repositioned centrally 6 feet from the front ditch and the position of the mat chosen by the first player. This does not, of course, apply to the first end, where the mat is always placed 6 feet from the back edge of the green.

The way a player stands on the mat (his stance) can vary from upright to crouch, but there is one law that a player must observe whether delivering the jack or, indeed, a bowl. At the moment of release the player must have one foot *on* or *over* the mat – in other words, entirely within the confines of the mat, although not necessarily in contact with it. Failure to observe this constitutes 'foot-faulting', and a bowl or jack delivered with a foot-fault can be declared 'dead' and therefore removed from the green.

This is a law that not only causes considerable controversy but is very difficult to judge. It is very rare indeed to see any player either pulled up or penalised for this offence, even though the law is quite clear.

Whatever the decision on the jack, the player who made the first cast will always remain the player to deliver the first bowl.

Remember: the first thing to do before the match commences is to toss a coin to see who starts. The winner has a choice – to place the mat and cast the jack or to give them to the opponent. There are a lot of bowlers who think that winning the toss means you automatically go first – but think about it. Sometimes it is better to have the last bowl! Thereafter the winner of the preceding scoring end goes first.

You are then normally allowed two trial ends (one each way) – although they are not counted as part of the game – in which your mat can be placed where you like (within the rules, of course!).

Movements – 'dead or live'

Bowls are described as being either 'dead' or 'live', and it's important to know when each applies.

First of all, let's deal with that 'live' bowl. Quite simply, it's a bowl that, when it comes to rest, is within the confines of the rink and not less than 15 yards from the front edge of the mat. In other words, it's in play. And it will remain in that state until the finish of the end unless legally played off the rink. A 'dead' bowl is a 'non-toucher' (*see* 'Touchers' section on page 37) that comes to rest either in the ditch or off the rink (that is, outside the boundaries). A bowl is not dead if it is carried up the green by a player inspecting the head. But don't drop it! In Federation circles you are not even allowed to put it down.

It is also as well to note that a bowl under EBA rules is not dead until it is entirely beyond the confines of the rink, whereas under EBF rules if it is touching the 'strings' it is declared dead.

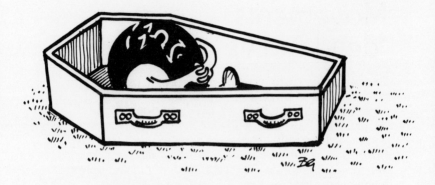

A jack can be live when it is taken into the ditch by a bowl but remains within the boundaries of the rink. The bowl will be either live or dead and will either remain (if live) or be removed (if dead).

An end can be declared dead for a number of reasons but this is usually when the jack has been knocked out of the rink. It can also be because either a bowl or bowls or the jack have been interfered with. In this case a skip will have four options:

1   to have the bowl (or jack) restored as nearly as possible to its original position
2   to let the disturbed bowl (or jack) remain where it finally rested
3   to have the bowl that disturbed the head declared dead
4   to call for the end to be replayed.

'Touchers'

If a bowl is a 'toucher', you will have to take into account its extra privileges.

The term 'toucher' is perhaps one of the best known in the game. It may have a different meaning under Association rules from that in the Federation or crown game, but in all cases a toucher is a bowl that touches the jack.

The toucher is really a modern invention; there is no mention of it in any of the early forms of bowls. The first time it appears is in Mitchell's *A Manual of Bowl-Playing*, devised by the Glasgow solicitor in 1865. But it is what sets Association bowling apart from the rest. So what is a toucher?

Quite simply, it's a bowl that on its course touches the jack, or falls over on to the jack before the next bowl comes to rest, while remaining within the confines of the rink. It can hit any number of bowls on its way, before the jack, but it's still a toucher. This bowl is then marked with chalk or sprayed from one of the new chalk-spray cans, and it remains a live bowl until it leaves the rink. Any other bowl is a 'non-toucher'.

Don't forget to do this, because if you don't mark a toucher (or 'nominate' it as such) before the next bowl comes to rest, it ceases to be a toucher.

The reason for nominating rather than marking a toucher may be that it is in danger of falling or is resting on another bowl and to mark it would only increase the probability of it making contact with another bowl. If it happens naturally, that's fine. But don't be the cause of it, especially if it gives you or your team the shot!

The law on this states that a bowl should be marked 'clearly with a chalkmark' and here you will see some differences. Some players put a cross, some a single line, while others add a little flourish. Whatever you do, remember to wet your piece of chalk – it's much easier to remove if you do.

However, a toucher whether played or knocked out of the rink becomes dead and must be removed to the bank like any other dead bowl. The only exception to this is a toucher that rebounds from the bank or another toucher in the ditch; these remain live.

Variations on a theme

All this may have sounded simple up to now, but there are several circumstances which do occur that need some explaining.

The first premise to remember is that a live bowl cannot itself interrupt play. If it displaces another bowl, that is a part of play. If, however, a non-toucher rebounds from the bank and hits a live bowl or jack, then the non-toucher, being of course dead, is removed, but any bowl or the jack which has been disturbed is then replaced as near as possible to its former location.

Should a player accidentally touch a live bowl – and this so often happens with a number of players milling about in the head or simply not keeping an eye open for bowls around their feet – then it must be put back to where it was, left where it now is or be declared dead. If a bowl, or the jack, is declared dead under these circumstances, the end is also dead and must be replayed.

It may not be a player on your rink that interrupts the play. It could be that a player from another rink, or even a bowl, disturbs a bowl or jack on your rink. You then have three choices: to agree to a repositioning of the bowl or jack affected; to declare the end dead and replay it in the same direction in the same order as before; if it is a bowl that has been displaced while in motion without having disturbed the head, the bowl is simply replayed.

Once a jack is in the ditch there can be no more touchers – so any bowl hitting the jack in the ditch, unless of course it's a previously marked toucher, has obviously interfered with the jack and it will have to be put back in its original position. In the case of the toucher the jack stays in its new position. The position of a live jack, and of a live bowl, should be marked on the bank with suitable markers.

There are ways to deal with the problem of deciding what constitutes a live or dead bowl if this is in dispute. Each rink has a boundary marker to indicate its confines. The rink can therefore be 'stringed' or an optical device such as a mirror can be used to determine whether or not a bowl or jack is completely over the line.

Fours play – the basis

The vast majority of games played in the UK will consist of team games – that is, either pairs, triples or fours, the game of fours not only forming the basis of the Association game but being the most popular too. So it is as well to examine what those games entail and the players required for each. In some cases the line-up may appear similar but players' roles within the team will be different, especially with the three-bowl triples game which entails the largest number of bowls used in any match – 18.

The basis of the Association game is fours play and the team consists of lead, second, third and skip, each playing two bowls. It must be remembered that in this game you have to remain in the positions stated on the card. (In the Federation game, which is based on triples, you can exchange places after each completed end.) The two leads will play first and bowl alternately, followed by seconds, thirds and finally skips.

The duties of a four are basically:

> *lead* – places mat and delivers jack
> *second* – keeps the score on card and scoreboard
> *third* – measures and agrees the number of shots
> *skip* – directs and takes the rap when defeated.

These are traditionally what the players in a fours team will do – besides bowling of course – but any player may undertake the duties specified if the skip (or captain of the rink) so decides. Usually, if the skip needs to leave the rink for any reason (and it should be for no longer than ten minutes and with the permission of the opposing skip) he will ask his third to take charge of the head. Any other player usually leaves immediately after he has delivered his two bowls and should be back well in time for the next end.

The player due to play the last bowl in any end is under no obligation to do so, but he must declare this to the opposition so that a declaration of the end can take place. Once he has done this, there is no going back.

Possession of the rink

With eight players on a rink (although the two skips will invariably be at the head) it can get a little crowded, so it's essential to keep track of who has 'possession of the rink'. This issue has raised passions over the years and many a bowler has complained about players who have allegedly contravened the laws.

The law is quite clear in that the team who are playing the bowl 'on the mat' are in possession of the rink and they should not be interfered with or have their attention distracted in any way by their opponents. This means that those who are not in the act of playing should stand behind the jack away from the head, or behind the mat. It also means no coughing, shuffling bowls or generally causing any disturbance likely to put the player on the mat off his delivery.

Emotions run high over the more exuberant players who run after their bowls and those who dare to show delight in a well-played bowl. To the etiquette-minded, embraces and joyful outbursts should be left on the football field. So watch out!

If a player transgresses once (and most of the time this is accidental), it's usually passed over. More than once and a polite request generally suffices, and apologies are always accepted – even if a certain degree of gamesmanship has been employed.

Defaults in fours

As in life, all is never quite simple in bowls and there are occasions when situations out of the normal occur in a fours game. Such circumstances are catered for in the laws.

It can happen that a player is absent from the rink at the start of a game. This may not be the player's fault, but there are rules to cover such a situation, which vary according to the type of match.

In the case of a single fours match where a club is represented by only one four, then unless all four players appear and are ready to play within the 30-minute maximum waiting period they must, according to the laws, forfeit the game.

However, in a domestic fours game where one player is absent, the three remaining players may play against another three but will lose a quarter of their shots total. There is also the possibility of three players playing against four, with the lead and second of the side with the absent player playing with three bowls each – but here again they face the forfeit of a quarter-shots deduction (fractions are taken into account!).

It gets a little complicated when this happens, but the theory is that with two players having three bowls each, the 25 per cent deduction is to 'even it up'. The lead in the team with the absent player is, in effect, playing the first of the missing player's bowls and the third is playing his second.

Irregularities in play

How often have you seen someone playing out of turn? Or delivering another player's bowl? Do you know what to do when this happens? An awful lot of bowlers don't!

Let's first consider playing out of turn. If a player goes out of turn then the skip of the opposing team has the right to stop the bowl in its course and it will then be returned for the player to play in the right order. If, however, it is unnoticed at the time, the opposing skip has two choices. He can leave the bowl where it is or he can declare the end dead, when it is restarted from the same end.

In the case of the player delivering the wrong bowl, which is quite easily done if there are bowls of the same make and size about and they have no distinguishing marks, it is a lot simpler. The wrong bowl is replaced with the right one after it has come to rest.

It is interesting to note that in both the situations described above, in a crown green game the bowls wrongly played would not be returned but forfeited!

When sets of rules are drawn up for any game they generally have to cover situations that are rare but can, and occasionally do, happen. It isn't very often that a player will need to change his bowls during a game; but what happens when he does?

You are not normally allowed to change your bowls during a game (although tennis, squash and badminton players can change their rackets, snooker players their cues, etc.) unless someone objects to them as being illegal, or they become unfit for play. This does not apply to the trial ends, although you must inform the opposing skip or the umpire if you intend to change them.

Another irregularity occurs when a player simply forgets to play his bowl. You might find this idea surprising, but it does happen. Quite simply, if you forget to play you have forfeited the right to play if a bowl has been played by each team before the mistake is discovered. If, however, before the mistake has been noticed a bowl has been delivered in the reverse order and the head has not been disturbed (i.e. a player plays before he should do), then the opponent plays two bowls in succession to restore the correct order. If the head has been disturbed then the opposing skip has the right either to leave the bowl where it is or to declare the end dead.

Outdoor bowls can sometimes be a chancy business if the weather decides to play up, and in this case there can often be an interruption in play. If an end in progress is abandoned and not completed, when the game is resumed it will be with the scores as they were when it was abandoned and as if the end had never been started.

If, however, when the game is resumed, perhaps on another day, and any of the original players is unable to be present, then one substitute is allowed, providing he is a member of the same club.

End results – scoring

Nothing could be simpler than the scoring system of bowls – honest!

The winner of an end is the player or team whose bowl(s) are nearest the jack. The number of shots depends on how many of one player's or team's bowls are nearer the jack than the opponents'. In other words, if you have the bowl nearest the jack but the next one is that of your opponents, you score one. If you have two closer than the nearest bowl of your opponent, you score two – and so on.

In the game of fours with each player having two bowls, the maximum score is therefore eight. This also applies to the game of four-bowl pairs. In singles, whether the maximum score is two or four will depend on whether it is a two-bowl or a four-bowl game. Triples is different again. In triples, where each of the three players has three bowls, the maximum is therefore nine – the highest individual end score in bowls.

An end technically finishes when the last bowl to be played has come to rest, but there is a provision for a bowl that looks as if it may fall and could become shot. The team to whom the bowl belongs is allowed 30 seconds before either team may take the count or measure.

Determining how many shots a team or individual has scored is usually the job of the third player in fours, the second player in triples, the lead in pairs or split between the two individual players in singles.

Some shots are quite obvious and will be immediately conceded, but if the two players determining the number of shots can't agree, the shot(s) in dispute will then have to be measured. (What usually happens is that the side with the count will say something like, 'I fancy two, perhaps three on a measure', and will receive the reply, 'Well, definitely one but you'll need to measure for the other two.')

There is no laid-down principle of who measures for shots or, indeed, who actually asks for them. It is usually the one who wants them that takes the initiative, but when it's an obvious case the opponent will concede and move those bowls out of the head that they think are counting.

No measuring is allowed until the end is finished; when doing so, all measurements are taken to the nearest point of bowl or jack, usually from the jack to the bowl in question. If a bowl is in a position where it is resting on another and the bowl it is resting on has to be moved, steps must be taken to prevent the bowl in question from falling (by using 'wedges'). Normally a flexible measure of an approved pattern will be used, and in close measures callipers are used to determine the result.

Measuring has been described as an art and should certainly be carried out with care and precision whether done by players, by a marker or by an umpire.

Sometimes neither side will score a shot because both teams' nearest bowls are equidistant from the jack and no degree of measuring can separate them. In this case no score (or 'nought') for each team will be recorded on the scorecards and the end declared 'drawn'. What is important, to avoid confusion with a 'dead end', is to note that this particular end has been played, has reached a conclusion and has been put on the card.

One law change that came into being in the 1970s is the playing of the last bowl. The player with the last bowl is under no obligation to play it but must declare to his opponent if he is forfeiting this right before the count can begin and the head is subsequently 'broken up'.

The laws state, somewhat ambiguously, that no bowls or jack should be moved until the skips have agreed the number of shots. But as the skip is down the other end when the decision on shots is taking place, this might

seem strange. So the threes agree the number of shots and indicate the score (or count) to the skips. The seconds then record this on the scorecard and scoreboard, agreeing before doing so, and the lead of the team winning the end places the mat for the next end to begin.

Scoring – nothing could be simpler. For each of your bowls that is nearer to the jack than the nearest of your opponents, count one shot! And remember the cardinal rule: *'If in doubt – measure out.'* Easy, isn't it?

Game decisions

There are certain rules that come into force at the conclusion of a game and determine the result. These fall into three categories.

In the case of a game that is part of a knockout competition and therefore comes under the heading of 'games played on one occasion', the result is determined by the player(s) who has scored the highest number of shots (or in the case of singles, whatever was the required number, invariably 21). In the case of games in a series it will be the player, team or side with the largest number of winning games, or the highest net score of shots, or whatever governs the tournament. Points may be awarded to indicate a team's success.

It could then come down to a combination of those factors and you could have a situation where both sides finish equal on all counts. If it is necessary to have a winner, an extra end(s) can be played to give a result.

An important factor to remember is that the game has officially finished and a result given. So if any further ends are started, it is a new game and players must toss a coin to determine who has the right to decide who plays first, and the end must be played from where the previous end was completed.

Undue influences

When formulating a set of laws for any game, allowances have to be made for situations that could well arise at any time, even if in practice they do not do so. The Laws of the Game of bowls therefore include a section that deals with 'oddities'.

Obviously, illness can strike at any time and a player may have to leave the green because he feels unwell, or indeed for some other reason. If that means the player is unable to continue, a substitute can be used, who must be a member of the club or team concerned. He can play only at lead, second or third so if it's the skip who is taken ill then the present third steps into the skip's shoes.

Remember that if a player leaves the green (for a 'call of nature', for instance), he must take no more than ten minutes.

In the case of competitions, the pair, triple or rink who play in the first round comprise the 'nominated team'. After that, any player who replaces another is then the 'substitute', and a single substitution is all that is allowed. However, the original player can come back in at any time because he was part of the nominated team.

How often have you seen a more experienced player showing a newcomer to the game the line to take the jack by standing in a certain position and indicating that 'bowling to his feet' will achieve the objective? Sometimes a cloth or handkerchief is used for the purpose. But what does the law say on this?

It says that you may not place any object to assist play *on* the green, or on a bowl, the jack or the bank. Note the key-word *on*. This obviously does not stop the skip or any other player indicating with a hand or cloth *above* the green.

I have heard of dogs invading bowling greens and playing chase-the-bowl, and even of a cheeky seagull who thought the jack was a tasty morsel. I'll certainly never forget the courageous squirrel who took to the green at Worthing's Beach House Park during a Middleton Cup final and, some say (supporters of the losing team?), won the match. But do you know the official procedure to follow in such cases?

The rule is that if the jack or bowls are disturbed by invaders – and that includes the wind – the end is declared dead unless the moved objects can be restored to their original positions to the agreement of the two skips.

The final part of the laws of bowls deals with the duties of markers and umpires, but just before that there is a tailpiece to the 'oddities' section regarding spectators. This states that spectators – that is, those not engaged in the game in progress – should stand clear of the play, preserve an attitude of complete neutrality and do nothing to disturb the participating players. All this sounds grand in theory but, as we all know, it is not so easy in practice. Given reasonable standards of behaviour, however, there are usually few complaints about a little good-natured support.

All concerned had better watch out on another point – no gambling at the clubs! Betting and gambling are not allowed in the flat green game within the grounds of any constituent club, so an alternative venue must be found. Gambling is an essential part of the fun of the crown green game and, from what I've seen, is enjoyed just as much on the flat.

Doing your duty

At some time during the year a bowls club member will almost certainly be asked to mark a game for fellow members, so it's important to know what to do and what you'll need to fulfil the task required.

The first prerequisite is a knowledge of the laws!
A marker should obviously have a piece of chalk or a chalk-spray for marking touchers, and a good measure. Before the game the marker will check that all the measurements of the rink and the players' bowls are legal. During play he will be required to centre and place the jack and check that it is within the limits. The marker doesn't have to wait for an objection.
Players will ask many questions during a game – 'How short was my last bowl?' or 'How many shots am I

holding?' – and the marker should answer specifically – 'Your last bowl was x feet short or through,' as the case may be, or 'You are holding two shots.'

There is a great deal of conjecture as to how much information a marker should give. Technically he should not elaborate or supply information not asked for, but this often presents him with a dilemma. If asked the question, 'Am I holding two shots?' when he knows that the player actually holds three, should the marker reply simply, 'Yes', or should he qualify this by saying, 'Actually, you are holding three'? It has been argued that by simply saying 'Yes' the marker is fulfilling his remit, and that by telling the player he is holding three he is overstepping what is required. You must decide for yourself what you think is fair.

It is the marker's job to chalk all touchers, and this is best done immediately the bowl comes to rest, although many will wait until the next player has delivered so as not to distract him.

The marker also measures all disputed shots and keeps the scorecard.

The duties of an umpire are very similar; he is really there to supply backing for the marker and to act as final decision-maker should a dispute arise.

Stamping of bowls

The stamping of bowls has provided many a talking point among bowlers in recent years, particularly when the EIBA abolished it for indoor play. But bowls manufacturers have always maintained that changes do take place in the character of a bowl over a period of years. Exactly when this happens is difficult to define, but manufacturers argue strongly that all bowls should be tested after a given period. Cynics argue that bowls testing means extra revenue for the manufacturers, and that this is the main reason they fight to save it.

What is fact is that all bowls should have a bias not less than the Master Bowl and should bear an official imprint of the WBB. If this stamp becomes illegible, it must be restamped. Bowls used outdoors are required to be retested only every ten years if you play at international level.

If you discover that an opponent's bowls are not valid in any way, you are legally entitled to demand that they are changed – albeit that this can be a little embarrassing at times.

Different codes

In the UK there are three main versions (codes) of the bowls game – Association, Federation and crown green. This can be further split into indoor and outdoor, and variations of indoor such as short mat. This book has set out to advise players mainly following the Association code, although reference is made to Federation variations, but it does not touch on crown green as this is a subject on its own.

The Association game, which is played in all four home countries (England, Ireland, Scotland and Wales) and throughout the world, plays to rules set out by the WBB, the governing body for the game worldwide, with certain domestic changes. The Federation game is followed by some thirteen counties of the North-East and East Anglia regions of England.

While there are many clubs who will play only the Association code, and a small number who will play only Federation, most clubs will play both codes where appropriate. The English Bowling Federation was established in the mid 1920s and its version is basically a two-wood game with a rink of players counted as three, not four as in Association rules.

The Federation code differs from that of the Association game in the following particulars.

1 The EBF does not recognise 'touchers'.
2 A jack in the ditch is 'live', whilst a bowl is 'dead'.
3 Bowls are taken into the count only if within 6 feet of the jack.
4 At the first end the front edge of the mat must be 6 feet from the ditch, and afterwards not more than 12 feet nor less than 6. Objection to the position must be made before the first bowl is delivered.
5 Players may change positions at the completion of any end.

6 In rinks (three players), the lead and the No. 2 can visit the head only after either eight or 12 bowls (two-bowl or three-bowl triples) have been delivered.

7 The jack or bowl is 'dead' on or over the dividing string.

8 In circumstances where three players have to play against two, the order of play will be: lead, lead, No. 2, repeated as necessary, followed by the skips.

Etiquette

Bowls is, perhaps, one of the most sociable games that you can play – its very pace allows for the establishment of friendships, which often can be enduring. To many, that's what gives the game its special charm. Its unwritten code of conduct (etiquette – 'conventional rules of manners') ensures that one bowler never seeks to have an unfair advantage over another, and on the green (as indeed happens in national competitions) all players are regarded as equals. It is a fact that the present generation of bowlers can thank the pioneers of the game for the many unwritten laws that still exist today. Proceedings always begin with friendly handshakes and introductions that quickly put players on first-name terms.

The guiding principle to all bowlers, and particularly to beginners, is that they should never do anything, on or off the green, that does not uphold the tradition or dignity of the game.

There will be bowlers who show impatience if you take too much time on the mat; there will be talkers, whistlers, those who hum indistinguishable melodies and those who find it impossible to keep still. There will also be those who are 'experts' on greenkeeping and on bowls in general. That's because bowls, like all walks of life, is made up of every variety of the human species and you must learn to deal with them all. The best you can do is to observe certain principles to ensure that you, at least, are the perfect player!

- Always be on time for matches and dressed in the correct attire.

- Stand still and remain quiet when other players are about to deliver, and always remember that only the player on the mat can ask for instructions from their skips ('possession of the rink').

- Remain behind the mat or the head when it is not your turn to play.

- Always try to keep to the rink that you are playing on – don't wander.

- Remember when outdoors on a sunny day that shadows can be cast.

- Avoid obscuring rink markers or boundary pegs.

- Pay attention to what is going on during the game, especially to your skip's instructions.

- Always be prepared to admit a lucky shot ('fluke') and never pretend that it was intended when you know it wasn't.

- If you follow a bowl after delivery, keep within the rules and try not to obscure your opponent's view of the bowl running up the green.

- When a skip decides on a firing shot it is a good idea to stand back and make sure that all players know so that they can avoid any bowls that 'fly about' in the head.

- Never openly criticise other players and always try to appear to be enjoying the game – despite your misfortunes!

- Avoid wasting time arguing which is shot. If there is any doubt, suggest to the person asking for the shot that they get down and measure, or offer to do it yourself.

Players often openly applaud the good shots of an opposition player, but there are mixed feelings on this, even at international level. It takes a player with a truly good nature to do this genuinely, and it is really up to the individual. However, you should always encourage players from your own team, whatever the circumstances. You will often hear, especially when anyone has been soundly beaten by someone they considered of inferior quality, that they played 'well above themselves' or note the remark, 'He'll never play as well as that again.' The fact is that, no matter how good a player is, he will always meet with defeat at some point. Bowls is very much a game of the day. Just remember that a player who has played extremely well has only reproduced the form he is capable of.

Remember, a good loser is a player who appears to have accepted his defeat with the best possible grace – even if inwardly seething!

ENGLISH BOWLING ASSOCIATION

The LAWS of the GAME
GOVERNING OUTDOOR BOWLS IN ENGLAND

As formulated by the World Bowls Board *(Laws revised 1992)*

11th EDITION

It should be appreciated that no code of laws governing a game has yet achieved such perfection as to cope with every situation. The code of laws governing bowls is no exception. Unusual incidents not definitely provided for in the laws frequently occur. It is well, therefore, to remember that the laws have been framed in the belief that true sportsmanship will prevail: that in the absence of any express rule commonsense will find a way to complete a happy solution to a knotty problem.

Amended Laws: 1(a) (j); 6(b); 8; 9(a) (b) (d); 38(a); 48; 66; 68; 69; 72(a); 73(a).

THE LAWS OF THE GAME

DEFINITIONS

1. (a) "Controlling Body" means the body having immediate control of the conditions under which a match is played. The order shall be: (i) The World Bowls Board, (ii) The National Bowling Authority, (iii) Divisions within National Authorities, (iv) The Club on whose Green the Match is played.

(b) "Skip" means the Player, who, for the time being, is in charge of the head on behalf of the team.

(c) "Team" means either a Four, Triples or a Pair.

(d) "Side" means any agreed number of Teams, whose combined scores determine the results of the match.

●●●

(e) "Four" means a team of four players whose positions in order of playing are named, Lead, Second, Third, Skip.
(f) "Bowl in Course" means a bowl from the time of its delivery until it comes to rest.
(g) "End" means the playing of the Jack and all the bowls of all the opponents in the same direction on a rink.
(h) "Head" means the Jack and such bowls as have come to rest within the boundary of the rink and are not dead.
(I) "Mat Line" means the edge of the Mat which is nearest to the front ditch. From the centre of the Mat Line all necessary measurements to Jack or bowls shall be taken.
(j) "Master Bowl" means a bowl which has been approved by the W.B.B. as having the minimum bias required, as well as in all other respects complying with the Laws of the Game and is engraved with the words "Master Bowl". (i) A Standard Test Bowl of the same bias as the Master Bowl shall be kept in the custody of each National Authority. (ii) A Standard Test Bowl shall be provided for the use of each official Licensed Tester.
(k) "Jack High" means that the nearest portion of the Bowl referred to is in line with and at the same distance from the Mat Line as the nearest portion of the Jack.
(I) "Pace of Green" means the number of seconds taken by a bowl from the time of its delivery to the moment it comes to rest, approximately 30 yards (27.43 metres) from the Mat Line.
(m) "Displaced" as applied to a Jack or Bowl means "disturbed" by any agency that is not sanctioned by these laws.
(n) A set of Bowls means four Bowls all of a matched set which are of the same manufacture and are of the same size, weight, colour, bias and where applicable serial number and engraving.

THE GREEN

2. The Green – Area and Surface The Green should form a square of not less than 120 feet (36.58 metres) and not more than 132 feet (40.23 metres) a side. It shall have a suitable natural playing surface which shall be level. It shall be provided with suitable boundaries in the form of a ditch and bank.
3. The Ditch The Green shall be surrounded by a ditch which shall have a holding surface not injurious to bowls and be free from obstacles. The ditch shall be not less than 8 inches (203 mm) nor more than 15 inches (381 mm) wide and it shall be not less than 2 inches (51 mm) nor more than 8 inches (203 mm) below the level of the green.
4. Banks The bank shall be not less than 9 inches (229 mm) above the level of the green, preferably upright, or alternatively at an angle of not more than 35 degrees from the perpendicular. The surface of the face of the bank shall be non-injurious to bowls. No steps likely to interfere with play shall be cut in the banks.
5. Division of the Green The Green shall be divided into spaces called rinks, each not more than 19 feet (5.79 metres), nor less than 18 feet (5.48 metres), wide. They shall be numbered consecutively, the centre line of each rink being marked on the bank at each end by a wooden peg or other suitable device. The four corners of the rinks shall be marked by pegs made of wood, or other suitable material, painted white and fixed to the face of the bank and flush therewith or alternatively fixed on the bank not more than four inches (102 mm) back from the face thereof. The corner pegs shall be connected by a green thread drawn tightly along the surface of the green, with sufficient loose thread to reach the corresponding pegs on the face or surface of the bank, in order to define the boundary of the rink.

White pegs or discs shall be fixed on the side banks to indicate a clear distance of 76 feet (23.16 metres) from the ditch on the line of play. Under no circumstances shall the boundary thread be lifted while the bowl is in motion. The boundary pegs of an outside rink shall be placed at least two feet (61 cm) from the side ditch.
6. Permissible Variations of Laws 2 and 5 (a) National Authorities may admit greens not longer than 44 yards (40.23 metres) nor shorter than 33 yards (30.17 metres) in the direction of play.
(b) For domestic play the Green may be divided into Rinks, not less than 14 feet (4.27 metres) nor more than 19 feet (5.79 metres) wide. National Authorities may dispense with the use of boundary threads. **(E.B.A. RULING:** *For play in the National Championships and National Competitions, the minimum width of a rink may be 16 feet (4.88 metres). Boundary threads may be dispensed with for play in England).*
(c) National Authorities may approve artificial surfaces for domestic play.

MAT, JACK, BOWLS, FOOTWEAR

7. Mat The Mat shall be of a definite size, namely 24 inches (61 cm) long and 14 inches (35.6 cm) wide.
8. Jack The Jack shall be round and white or yellow in colour, with a diameter of not less than 2-15/32nd inches (63 mm), nor more than 2-17/32nd inches (64 mm), and not less than 8 ounces (227 gr), nor more than 10 ounces (283 gr), in weight. **(E.B.A. RULING:** *A jack, weighing not less than 13½ ounces (382 gr) nor more than 16 ounces (453 gr), may be used by mutual consent on an outdoor green having an artificial surface).*
9. Bowls (a) (i) Bowls shall be made of wood, rubber or composition and shall be black or brown in colour, and each bowl of the set shall bear the member's individual and distinguishing mark on each side. The provision relating to the distinguishing mark on each side of the bowl need not apply other than in International Matches, World Bowls Championships and Commonwealth Games.

Bowls made of wood (lignum vitae) shall have a maximum diameter of 5¼ ins (134 mm) and a minimum diameter of 4⁹∕₁₆ ins (116 mm) and the weight shall not exceed 3lbs 8oz (1.59 kg). Loading of bowls made of wood is strictly prohibited. (ii) For all International and Commonwealth Games Matches, a bowl made of rubber or composition shall have a maximum diameter of 5⅛ ins (131 mm) and a minimum diameter of 4⁹∕₁₆ ins (116 mm) and the weight shall not exceed 3lb 8oz (1.59 kg).

Subject to bowls bearing a current stamp of the Board and/or a current stamp of a Member National Authority and/or a current stamp of the B.I.B.C. and provided they comply with the Board's Laws, they may be used in all matches controlled by the Board or by any Member National Authority.

Notwithstanding the aforegoing provisions, any Member National Authority may adopt a different scale of weights and sizes of bowls to be used in matches under its own control – such bowls may not be validly used in International Matches, World Championships, Commonwealth Games or other matches controlled by the Board if they differ from the Board's Laws, and unless stamped with a current stamp of the Board or any Member National Authority or the B.I.B.C. (iii) The Controlling Body may, at its discretion, supply and require players to temporarily affix an adhesive marking to their bowls in any competition game. Any temporary marking under this Law shall be regarded as part of the bowl for all purposes under these laws.
(b) Bias of Bowls The Master Bowl shall have a Bias approved by the World Bowls Board. A Bowl shall have a Bias

●●●

not less than that of the Master Bowl, and shall bear the imprint of the Stamp of the International Bowling Board/World Bowls Board, or that of its National Authority. National Authorities may adopt a standard which exceeds the bias of the Master Bowl. To ensure accuracy of bias and visibility of stamp, all bowls shall be re-tested and re-stamped at least once every ten years, or earlier if the date of the stamp is not clearly legible. **(E.B.A. RULING**: *As from 1st January 1986 the re-stamping of composition bowls for competitive and domestic play in England is dispensed with. Bowls must, however, bear a legible stamp for 1985 or later, and can continue to be used without stamping until such time as the stamp becomes illegible.)*

(c) Bowls Failing Test If a Bowl in the hands of a Licensed Tester has been declared as not complying with 9(b), it shall be altered, if possible, so as to comply, before being returned. The owner of the Bowl shall be responsible for the expense involved.

If the Bowl cannot be altered to comply with 9(a) and (b) any current official stamp appearing thereon shall be cancelled prior to its return. The stamp shall be cancelled by the Tester by stamping an X over any current official stamp.

Bowls submitted for testing must be in sets of four.

(d) Objection to Bowls A challenge may be lodged by an opposing player and/or the official Umpire, and/or the Controlling Body.

A challenge or any intimation thereof shall not be lodged with any opposing player during the progress of a Match.

A challenge may be lodged with the Umpire at any time during a Match, provided the Umpire is not a Player in that or any other match of the same competition.

If a challenge be lodged it shall be made not later than ten minutes after the completion of the final end in which the Bowl was used.

Once a challenge is lodged with the Umpire, it cannot be withdrawn.

The challenge shall be based on the grounds that the bowl does not comply with one or more of the requirements set out in Law 9(a) and 9(b).

The Umpire shall request the user of the bowl to surrender it to him for forwarding to the Controlling Body. If the owner of the challenged bowl refuses to surrender it to the Umpire, the Match shall thereupon be forfeited to the opponent. The user or owner, or both, may be disqualified from playing in any match controlled or permitted by the Controlling Body, so long as the bowl remains untested by a licensed tester.

On receipt of the bowl, the Umpire shall take immediate steps to hand it to the Secretary of the Controlling Body, who shall arrange for a table test to be made as soon as practicable, and in the presence of a representative of the Controlling Body.

If a table test be not readily available, and any delay would unduly interfere with the progress of the competition, then, should an approved green testing device be available, it may be used to make an immediate test on the Green. If a green test be made it shall be done by, or in the presence of, the Umpire over a distance of not less than 70 feet (21.35 metres). The comparison shall be between the challenged bowl and the Standard W.B.B. Test Bowl, or if it be not readily available then a Bowl bearing a current stamp, of similar size or nearly so, should be used.

The decision of the Umpire, as a result of the test, shall be final and binding for that match.

The result of the subsequent table test shall not invalidate the decision given by the Umpire on the green test.

If a challenged bowl, after an official table test, be found to comply with all the requirements of Law 9(a) and (b), it shall be returned to the user or owner.

If the challenged bowl be found not to comply with Law 9(a) and (b), the match in which it was played shall be forfeited to the opponent.

If the owner refuses his consent, and demands the return of his bowl, any current official stamp appearing thereon shall be cancelled prior to its return.

(e) Alteration to Bias A player shall not alter, or cause to be altered, other than by an official bowl tester, the bias of any bowl, bearing the imprint of the official stamp of the Board, under penalty of suspension from playing for a period to be determined by the Council of the National Authority, of which his club is a member. Such suspension shall be subject to confimation by the Board, or a committee thereof appointed for that purpose, and shall be operative among all Authorities in membership with the Board.

10. Footwear Players, Umpires and Markers shall wear white, brown or black smooth-soled heel-less footwear while playing on the green or acting as Umpires or Markers.

ARRANGING A GAME

11. General form and duration A game of bowls shall be played on one rink or on several rinks. It shall consist of a specified number of shots or ends, or shall be played for any period of time as previously arranged.

The ends of the game shall be played alternately in opposite directions excepting as provided in Laws 38, 42, 44, 46 and 47.

12. Selecting the rinks for play When a match is to be played, the draw for the rinks to be played on shall be made by the skips or their representatives.

In a match for a trophy or where competing skips have previously been drawn, the draw to decide the numbers of the rinks to be played on shall be made by the visiting skips or their representatives.

No player in a competition or match shall play on the same rink on the day of such competition or match before play commences under penalty of disqualification.

This law shall not apply in the case of open Tournaments.

13. Play arrangements Games shall be organised in the following play arrangements: (a) As a single game. (b) As a team game. (c) As a sides game. (d) As a series of single games, team games, or side games. (e) As a special tournament of games.

14. A single game shall be played on one rink of a Green as a single-handed game by two contending players, each playing two, three or four bowls singly and alternately.

15. (a) A Pairs game by two contending teams of two players called lead and skip according to the order in which they play, and who at each end shall play four bowls alternately, the leads first, then the skips similarly.

●●

(For other than International and Commonwealth Games, players in a Pairs game may play two, three or four bowls each, as previously arranged by the Controlling Body).

(b) A Pairs game by two contending teams of two players called Lead and Skip according to the order in which they play, and who at each end shall play four bowls and may play alternatively in the following order: Lead 2 bowls, Skip 2 bowls, then repeat this order of play. *(The English Bowling Association will not adopt this method of play for any Pairs competition under their direct control. If clubs or county associations wish to play this method of Pairs game they are at liberty to do so, providing it is not part of a national competition).*

16. A Triples game by two contending teams of three players, who shall play two or three bowls singly and in turn, the leads playing first.

17. A Fours game by two contending teams of four players, each member playing two bowls singly and in turn.

18. A side game shall be played by two contending sides, each composed of an equal number of teams/players.

19. Games in series shall be arranged to be played on several and consecutive occasions as: **(a)** A series or sequence of games organised in the form of an eliminating competition, and arranged as Singles, Pairs, Triples or Fours. **(b)** A series or sequence of side matches organised in the form of a league competition, or an eliminating competition, or of inter-association matches.

20. A special tournament of games: Single games and team games may also be arranged in group form as a special tournament of games in which the contestants play each other in turn, or they may play as paired-off teams of players on one or several greens in accordance with a common time-table, success being adjudged by the number of games won, or by the highest net score in shots in accordance with the regulations governing the Tournament.

21. For International Matches, World Bowls and Commonwealth Games, including British Isles Championships, in matches where played. (i) Singles shall be 25 shots up (shots in excess of 25 shall not count), four bowls each player, played alternately; (ii) Pairs shall be 21 ends, four bowls each player, played alternately; (iii) Triples shall be 18 ends, three bowls each player, played alternately; (iv) Fours shall be 21 ends, two bowls each player, played alternately; **(E.B.A. RULING**: *Singles play under EBA jurisdiction shall be 21 shots up).*

PROVIDED that Pairs, Triples and Fours may be of a lesser number of ends, but in the case of Pairs and Fours there shall not be less than 18 ends and in the case of Triples not less than 15 ends, subject in all cases to the express approval of the Board as represented by its most senior officer present. If there be no officer of the Board present at the time, the decision shall rest with the "Controlling Body" as defined in Law 1. Any decision to curtail the number of ends to be played shall be made before the commencement of any game, and such decision shall only be made on the grounds of climatic conditions, inclement weather or shortage of time to complete a programme.

22. Awards Cancelled; see By-Laws after Rule 73 under heading "Professional Bowler".

STARTING THE GAME

23. (a) Trial ends Before start of play in any competition, match or game, or on the resumption of an unfinished competition, match or game on another day, not more than one trial end each way shall be played.

(b) Tossing for opening play The captains in a side game or skips in a team shall toss to decide which side or team shall play first, but in all singles games the opponents shall toss, the winner of the toss to have the option of decision. In the event of a tied (no score) or a dead end, the first to play in the tied end or dead end shall again play first.

In all ends subsequent to the first the winner of the preceding scoring end shall play first.

24. Placing the Mat At the beginning of the first end the player to play first shall place the centre line of the mat lengthwise on the centre line of the rink, the front edge of the mat to be six feet (1.84 metres) from the ditch. (Where ground sheets are in use they shall be placed with the back edge six feet (1.84 metres) from the ditch. The mat at the first and every subsequent end shall be placed at the back edge of the sheet – the mat's front edge being six feet (1.84 metres) from the ditch).

25. The Mat and its replacement After play has commenced in any end the mat shall not be moved from its first position.

If the mat be displaced during the process of an end it shall be replaced as near as practicable in the same position.

If the mat be out of alignment with the centre line of the rink it may be straightened at any time during the end.

After the last bowl in each end has come to rest in play, or has sooner become dead, the mat shall be lifted and placed wholly beyond the face of the rear bank. Should the mat be picked up by a player before the end has been completed, the opposing player shall have the right of replacing the mat in its original position.

26. The Mat and Jack in subsequent ends In all subsequent ends the front edge of the mat shall be not less than six feet (1.84 metres) from the rear ditch and the front edge not less than 76 feet (23.16 metres) from the front ditch, and on the centre line of the rink of play.

(b) Should the jack be improperly delivered under Law 30, the opposing player may then move the mat in the line of play, subject to clause (a) above, and deliver the jack, but shall not play first. Should the jack be improperly delivered twice by each player in any end, it shall not be delivered again in that end, but shall be centred so that the front of the jack is a distance of six feet (1.84 metres) from the opposite ditch, and the mat placed at the option of the first to play.

If, after the jack is set at regulation length from the ditch (6 feet, 1.84 metres) and both players each having improperly delivered the jack twice, that end is then made dead, the winner of the preceding scoring end shall deliver the jack when the end is played anew.

(c) No one shall be permitted to challenge the legality of the original position of the mat after the first to play has delivered the first bowl.

27. Stance on Mat A player shall take his stance on the mat, and at the moment of delivering the Jack or his Bowl, shall have one foot remaining entirely within the confines of the mat. The foot may be either in contact with, or over, the mat. Failure to observe this law constitutes foot-faulting.

28. Foot-faulting Should a player infringe the Law of foot-faulting the Umpire may, after having given a warning, have the bowl stopped and declared dead. If the bowl has disturbed the head, the opponent shall have the option of either resetting the head, leaving the head as altered or declaring the end dead.

29. Delivering the Jack The Player to play first shall deliver the Jack. If the Jack in its original course comes to rest at a distance of less than 2 yards (1.84 metres) from the opposite ditch, it shall be moved out to a mark at that distance so that the front of the Jack is six feet (1.84 metres) from the front ditch, with the nearest portion of the Jack to the mat line

●●

being six feet (1.84 metres) from the edge of the opposite ditch. (**E.B.A. RULING**: *If a mark has not been placed on the green the Jack shall be moved so that the front edge of the Jack is six feet (1.84 metres) from the front ditch, and centred*). If the Jack during its original course be obstructed or deflected by a neutral object or neutral person, or by a marker, opponent or member of the opposing team, it shall be redelivered by the same player, but if it be obstructed or deflected by a member of his own team, it shall be redelivered by the Lead of the opposing team, who shall be entitled to reset the mat.

30. Jack improperly delivered Should the Jack in any end be not delivered from a proper stance on the mat, or if it ends its original course in the ditch or outside the side boundary of the rink, or less than 70 feet (21.35 metres) in a straight line of play from the front edge of the mat, it shall be returned and the opposing player shall deliver the Jack but shall not play first.

The Jack shall be returned if it is improperly delivered, but the right of the player first delivering the Jack in that end, to play the first bowl of the end shall not be affected.

No one shall be permitted to challenge the legality of the original length of the Jack after the first to play has delivered the first bowl.

31. Variations to Laws 24, 26, 29 and 30 Notwithstanding anything contained in Laws 24, 26, 29 and 30, any National Authority may for domestic purposes, but not in any International Matches, World Bowls Championships or Commonwealth Games, vary any of the distances mentioned in these Laws.

MOVEMENT OF BOWLS

32. "Live" Bowl A Bowl which, in its original course on the Green, comes to rest within the boundaries of the rink, and not less than 15 yards (13.71 metres) from the front edge of the mat shall be accounted as a "Live" bowl and shall be in play.

33. "Touchers" A bowl which, in its original course on the green, touches the Jack, even though such bowl passes into the ditch within the boundaries of the rink, shall be counted as a "live" bowl and shall be called a "toucher". If after having come to rest a bowl falls over and touches the Jack before the next succeeding bowl is delivered, or if in the case of the last bowl of an end it falls and touches the Jack within the period of half a minute invoked under Law 53, such bowl shall also be a "toucher". No bowl shall be accounted a "toucher" by playing on to, or by coming into contact with, the Jack while the Jack is in the ditch. If a "toucher" in the ditch cannot be seen from the mat its position may be marked by a white or coloured peg about 2 inches (51 mm) broad placed upright on the top of the bank and immediately in line with the place where the "toucher" rests.

34. Marking a "Toucher" A "toucher" shall be clearly marked with a chalk mark by a member of the player's team. If, in the opinion of either Skip, or opponent in Singles, a "toucher" or a wrongly chalked bowl comes to rest in such a position that the act of making a chalk mark, or of erasing it, is likely to move the bowl or to alter the head, the bowl shall not be marked or have its mark erased but shall be "indicated" as a "toucher" or "non-toucher" as the case may be. If a bowl is not so marked or not so "indicated" before the succeeding bowl comes to rest it ceases to be a "toucher". If both Skips or opponents agree that any subsequent movement of the bowl eliminates the necessity for continuation of the "indicated" provision the bowl shall thereupon be marked or have the chalk mark erased as the case may be. Care should be taken to remove "toucher" marks from all bowls before they are played, but should a player fail to do so, and should the bowl not become a "toucher" in the end in play, the marks shall be removed by the opposing Skip or his deputy or marker immediately the bowl comes to rest unless the bowl is "indicated" as a "non-toucher" in circumstances governed by earlier provisions of this Law.

35. Movement of "Touchers" A "toucher" in play in the ditch may be moved by the impact of a jack in play or of another "toucher" in play, and also by the impact of a non-toucher which remains in play after the impact, and any movement of the "toucher" by such incidents shall be valid. However, should the non-toucher enter the ditch at any time after the impact, it shall be dead, and the "toucher" shall be deemed to have been displaced by a dead bowl and the provisions of Law 38(e) shall apply.

36. Bowl Accounted "Dead" (a) Without limiting the application at any other of these Laws, a bowl shall be accounted dead if it: (i) not being a "toucher", comes to rest in the ditch or rebounds on to the playing surface of the rink after contact with the bank or with the Jack or a "toucher" in the ditch, or (ii) after completing its original course, or after being moved as a result of play, it comes to rest wholly outside the boundaries of the playing surface of the rink, or within 15 yards (13.71 metres) of the front of the mat, or (iii) in its original course, pass beyond a side boundary of the rink on a bias which would prevent its re-entering the rink. (A bowl is not rendered "dead" by a player carrying it whilst inspecting the head).

(b) Skips or the Opponents in Singles shall agree on the question as to whether or not a bowl is "dead". Any member of either Team may request a decision from the Skips, but no Member shall remove any bowl prior to agreement by the Skips. Once their attention has been drawn to the matter, the Skips by agreement must make a decision. If they cannot reach agreement, the Umpire must make an immediate decision.

37. Bowl Rebounding Only "Touchers" rebounding from the face of the bank to the ditch or to the rink shall remain in play.

38. Bowl Displacement (a) Displacement by rebounding "non-toucher" – bowl displaced by a "non-toucher" rebounding from the bank shall be restored as near as possible to its original position, by a member of the opposing team or by the Marker.

(b) Displacement by participating player – if a bowl, while in motion or at rest on the green, or a "toucher" in the ditch, be interfered with, or displaced by one of the players, the opposing skip shall have the option of: (i) restoring the bowl as near as possible to its original position; (ii) letting it remain where it rests; (iii) declaring the bowl "dead"; (iv) or declaring the end dead.

(c) Displacement by a neutral object or neutral person (other than as provided in Clause (d) hereof): (i) of a bowl in its original course – if such a bowl be displaced within the boundaries of the rink of play without having disturbed the head, it shall be replayed. If it be displaced and it has disturbed the head, the skips, or the opponents in singles, shall reach agreement on the final position of the displaced bowl and on the replacement of the head, otherwise the end shall be dead. These provisions shall also apply to a bowl in its original course displaced outside the boundaries of the rink of play provided such bowl was running on a bias which would have enabled it to re-enter the rink. (ii) of a bowl at rest, or in motion as a result of play after being at rest – if such a bowl be displaced, the skips, or opponents in singles, shall come to an agreement as to the position of the bowl and of the replacement of any part of the head disturbed by the displaced bowl, otherwise the end shall be dead.

(d) Displacement inadvertently produced – if a bowl be moved at the time of it being marked or measured it shall be restored to its former position by an opponent. If such displacement is caused by a Marker or an Umpire, the Marker or Umpire shall replace the bowl.

(e) Displacement by dead bowl – if a "toucher" in the ditch be displaced by a dead bowl from the rink of play, it shall be restored to its original position by a player of the opposite team or by the marker.

39. "Line Bowls" A bowl shall not be accounted as outside any line unless it be entirely clear of it. This shall be ascertained by looking perpendicularly down upon the bowl or by placing a square on the green.

MOVEMENT OF JACK

40. A "Live" Jack in the Ditch A Jack moved by a bowl in play into the front ditch within the boundaries of the rink shall be deemed to be "live". It may be moved by the impact of a "toucher" in play and also by the impact of a "non-toucher" which remains in play after impact; any movement of the jack by such incidents shall be valid. However, should the "non-toucher" enter the ditch after impact, it shall be "dead" and the Jack shall be deemed to have been "displaced" by a "dead" bowl and the provisions of Law 48 shall apply. If the Jack in the ditch cannot be seen from the mat its position shall be marked by a "white" peg about 2 inches (51 mm) broad and not more than 4 inches (102 mm) in height, placed upright on top of the bank and immediately in line from the place where the Jack rests.

41. A Jack accounted "dead" Should the Jack be driven by a bowl in play and come to rest wholly beyond the boundary of the rink, i.e., over the bank, or over the side boundary, or into any opening or inequality of any kind in the bank, or rebound to a distance less than 61 feet (18.59 metres) in direct line from the centre of the front edge of the mat to the Jack in its rebounded position, it shall be accounted "dead".

("National Authorities have the option to vary the distance to which a Jack may rebound and still be playable for games other than International and Commonwealth Games.")

42. "Dead" End When the Jack is "dead" the end shall be regarded as a "dead" end and shall not be accounted as a played end even though all the bowls in that end have been played. All "dead" ends shall be played anew in the same direction unless both Skips or Opponents in Singles agree to play in the opposite direction.

After a "dead" end situation, the right to deliver the Jack shall always return to the player who delivered the original Jack.

43. Playing to a boundary Jack The Jack, if driven to the side boundary of the rink and not wholly beyond its limits, may be played to on either hand and, if necessary, a bowl may pass outside the side limits of the rink. A bowl so played, which comes to rest within the boundaries of the rink, shall not be accounted "dead".

If the Jack be driven to the side boundary line and comes to rest partly within the limits of the rink, a bowl played outside the limits of the rink and coming to rest entirely outside the boundary line, even though it has made contact with the Jack, shall be accounted "dead" and shall be removed to the bank by a member of the player's team.

44. A Damaged Jack In the event of a jack being damaged, the Umpire shall decide if another jack is necessary and, if so, the end shall be regarded as a "dead" end and another jack shall be substituted and the end shall be replayed anew.

45. A rebounding Jack If the jack is driven against the face of the bank and rebounds on to the rink, or after being played into the ditch, it be operated on by a "toucher", so as to find its way on to the rink, it shall be played to in the same manner as if it had never left the rink.

46. Jack displacement (a) *By a player* If the jack be diverted from its course while in motion on the green, or displaced while at rest on the green, or in the ditch, by any one of the players, the opposing skip shall have the jack restored to its former position, or allow it to remain where it rests and play the end to a finish, or declare the end "dead".

(b) *Inadvertently produced* If the jack be moved at the time of measuring by a player it shall be restored to its former position by an opponent.

47. Jack displaced by non-player (a) If the jack, whether in motion or at rest on the rink, or in the ditch, be displaced by a bowl from another rink, or by any object or by an individual not a member of the team, the two skips shall decide as to its original position, and if they are unable to agree, the end shall be declared "dead".

(b) If a jack be displaced by a marker or umpire it shall be restored by him to its original position of which he shall be the sole judge.

48. Jack displaced by "non-toucher" A jack displaced in the rink of play by a "non-toucher" rebounding from the bank shall be restored, or as near as possible, to its original position by a player of the opposing team or by the Marker in a Singles game. Should a jack, however, after having been played into the ditch, be displaced by a "dead bowl" it shall be restored to its marked position by a player of the opposing team or by the marker.

FOURS PLAY
The basis of the Game of Bowls is Fours Play

49. The rink and fours play (a) *Designation of players*. A team shall consist of four players, named respectively, lead, second, third and skip, according to the order in which they play, each playing two bowls.

(b) *Order of Play*. The leads shall play their two bowls alternately, and so on, each pair of players in succession to the end. No one shall play until his opponents' bowl shall have come to rest. Except under circumstances provided for in Law 63, the order of play shall not be changed after the first end has been played, under penalty of disqualification, such penalty involving the forfeiture of the match or game to the opposing team.

50. Possession of the Rink Possession of the rink shall belong to the team whose bowl is being played. The players in possession of the rink for the time being, shall not be interfered with, annoyed, or have their attention distracted in any way by their opponents.

As soon as each bowl shall have come to rest, possession of the rink shall be transferred to the other team, time being allowed for marking a "toucher".

51. Position of Players Players of each team not in the act of playing or controlling play, shall stand behind the jack and away from the head, or one yard (92 cm) behind the mat. As soon as the bowl is delivered, the skip or player directing, if in front of the jack shall retire behind it.

52. Players and their duties **(a)** The Skip shall have sole charge of his team, and his instructions shall be observed by his players. With the opposing skip he shall decide all disputed points, and when both agree their decision shall be final. If both skips cannot agree, the point in dispute shall be referred to, and considered by, an Umpire whose decision shall be final. A skip may at any time delegate his powers and any of his duties to other members of his team provided that such delegation is notified to the opposing skip.

(b) The third. The third player may have deputed to him the duty of measuring any and all disputed shots.

(c) The second. The second player shall keep a record of all shots scored for and against his team and shall at all times retain possession of the score card whilst play is in progress. He shall see that the names of all players are entered on the score card; shall compare his record of the game with that of the opposing second player as each end is declared, and at the close of the game shall hand his score card to his skip.

(d) The Lead. The Lead shall place the mat, and shall deliver the jack ensuring that the jack is properly centered before playing his first bowl.

(e) In addition to the duties specified in the preceding clauses, any player may undertake such duties as may be assigned to him by the skip in Clause 52(a) hereof.

RESULT OF END

53. "The shot" A shot or shots shall be adjudged by the bowl or bowls nearer to the jack than any bowl played by the opposing player or players.

When the last bowl has come to rest, half a minute shall elapse, if either team desires, before the shots are counted.

Neither jack nor bowls shall be moved until each skip has agreed to the number of shots, except in circumstances where a bowl has to be moved to allow the measuring of another bowl.

54. Measuring conditions to be observed No measuring shall be allowed until the end has been completed.

All measurements shall be made to the nearing point of each object. If a bowl requiring to be measured is resting on another bowl which prevents its measurement, the best available means shall be taken to secure its position, whereupon the other bowl shall be removed. The same course shall be followed where more than two bowls are involved, or where, in the course of measuring, a single bowl is in danger of falling or otherwise changing its position.

When it is necessary to measure to a bowl or jack in the ditch, and another bowl or jack on the green, the measurement shall be made with the ordinary flexible measure. Calipers may be used to determine the shot only when the bowls in question and the jack are on the same plane.

55. "Tie" – No shot When at the conclusion of play in any end the nearest bowl of each team is touching the jack, or is deemed to be equidistant from the jack, there shall be no score recorded. The end shall be declared "drawn" and shall be counted a played end.

56. Nothing in these Laws shall be deemed to make it mandatory for the last player to play his last bowl in any end, but he shall declare to his opponent or opposing skip his intention to refrain from playing it before the commencement of determining the result of the end and his declaration shall be irrevocable.

GAME DECISIONS

57. Games played on one occasion In the case of a single game or a team game or a side game played on one occasion, or at any stage of an eliminating competition, the victory decision shall be awarded to the player, team, or side of players producing at the end of the game, the higher total score of shot, or in the case of a "game of winning ends", a majority of winning ends.

58. Tournament games and games in series In the case of Tournament games or games in series, the victory decision shall be awarded to the player, team or side of players producing at the end of the tournament or series of contests, either the largest number of winning games or the highest net score of shots in accordance with the regulations governing the tournament or series of games.

Points may be used to indicate game successes.

Where points are equal, the aggregate shots scored against each team (or side) shall be divided into the aggregate shots it has scored. The team (or side) with the highest result shall be declared the winner.

59. Playing to a finish and possible drawn games If in an eliminating competition, consisting of a stated or agreed upon number of ends, it be found, when all the ends have been played, that the scores are equal, an extra end or ends shall be played until a decision has been reached.

The captains or skips shall toss and the winner shall have the right to decide who shall play first. The extra end shall be played from where the previous end was completed, and the mat shall be placed in accordance with Law 24.

DEFAULTS OF PLAYERS IN FOURS PLAY

60. Absentee players in any team or side **(a) In a single Fours game**, for a trophy, prize or other competitive award, where a club is represented by only one Four, each member of such Four shall be a bona fide member of the club. Unless all four players appear and are ready to play at the end of the maximum waiting period of 30 minutes, or should they introduce an ineligible player, then that team shall forfeit the match to the opposing team.

(b) In a domestic Fours game. Where, in a domestic Fours game the number of players cannot be accommodated in full teams of four players, three players may play against three players, but shall suffer the deduction of one fourth of the total sore of each team.

A smaller number of players than six shall be excluded from that game.

(c) In a Side game. If within a period of 30 minutes from the time fixed for the game, a single player is absent from one or both teams in a side game, whether a friendly club match or a match for a trophy, prize or other award, the game shall proceed, but in the defaulting team, the number of bowls shall be made up by the lead and second players playing three bowls each, but one-fourth of the total shots scored by each "four" playing three men shall be deducted from their score at the end of the game.

Fractions shall be taken into account.

(d) In a Side game. Should such default take place where more Fours than one are concerned, or where a Four has been disqualified for some other infringement, and where the average score is to decide the contest, the scores of the non-defaulting Fours only shall be counted, but such average shall, as a penalty in the case of the defaulting side, be arrived at by dividing the aggregate score of that side by the number of Fours that should have been played and not as in the case of the other side, by the number actually engaged in the game.

61. Play irregularities (a) Playing out of turn. When a player has played before his turn the opposing skip shall have the right to stop the bowl in its course and it shall be played in its proper turn, but in the event of the bowl so played, having moved or displaced the jack or bowl, the opposing skip shall have the option of allowing the end to remain as it is after the bowl so played, has come to rest, or having the end declared "dead".

(b) Playing the wrong bowl. A bowl played by mistake shall be replaced by the player's own bowl.

(c) Changing bowls. A player shall not be allowed to change his bowls during the course of a game, or in a resumed game, unless they be objected to, as provided in Law 9(d), or when a bowl has been so damaged in the course of play as, in the opinion of the Umpire, to render the bowl (or bowls) unfit for play.

(d) Omitting to play (i) If the result of an end has been agreed upon, or the head has been touched in the agreed process of determining the result, then a player who forfeits or has omitted to play a bowl, shall forfeit the right to play it. (ii) A player who has neglected to play a bowl in the proper sequence shall forfeit the right to play such bowl, if a bowl has been played by each team before such mistake was discovered. (iii) If before the mistake be noticed, a bowl has been delivered in the reversed order and the head has not been disturbed, the opponent shall then play two successive bowls to restore the correct sequence.

If the head has been disturbed Clause 61(a) shall apply.

62. Play Interruptions (a) Game Stoppages. When a game of any kind is stopped, either by mutual arrangement or by the Umpire, after appeal to him on account of darkness or the conditions of the weather, or any other valid reason, it shall be resumed with the scores as they were when the game stopped. An end commenced, but not completed, shall be declared null.

(b) Substitutes in a resumed game. If in a resumed game any one of the four original players be not available, one substitute shall be permitted as stated in Law 63 below. Players, however, shall not be transferred from one team to another.

INFLUENCES AFFECTING PLAY

63. Leaving the Green If during the course of a side Fours, Triples or Pairs game a player has to leave the green owing to illness, or other reasonable cause, his place shall be filled by a substitute, if in the opinion of both skips (or failing agreement by them, then in the opinion of the Controlling Body) such substitution is necessary. Should the player affected be a skip, his duties and position in a Fours game shall be assumed by the third player, and the substitute shall play either as a lead, second or third. In the case of Triples the substitute may play either as lead or second but not as skip and in the case of Pairs the substitute shall play as lead only. Such substitute shall be a member of the club to which the team belongs. In domestic play National Authorities may decide the position of any substitute

If during the course of a single-handed game, a player has to leave the green owing to illness, or reasonable cause, the provision of Law 62(a) shall be observed.

No player shall be allowed to delay the play by leaving the rink or team, unless with the consent of his opponent, and then only by a period not exceeding ten minutes.

Contravention of this Law shall entitle the opponent or opposing team to claim the game or match.

64. Objects on the Green Under no circumstances, other than as provided in Laws 29, 33 and 40, shall any extraneous object to assist a player be placed on the green, or on the bank, or on the jack, or on a bowl or elsewhere.

65. Unforeseen incidents If during the course of play, the position of the jack or bowls be disturbed by wind, storm, or by any neutral object the end shall be declared "dead", unless the skips are agreed as to the replacement of jack or bowls.

DOMESTIC ARRANGEMENTS

66. In addition to any matters specifically mentioned in these Laws, National Authorities may, in circumstances dictated by climate or other local conditions, make such other regulations as are deemed necessary and desirable, but such regulations must be submitted to the W.B.B. for approval. For this purpose the Board shall appoint a Committee to be known as the "Laws Committee" with powers to grant approval or otherwise to any proposal, such decision being valid until the proposal is submitted to the Board for a final decision.

67. Local Arrangements Constituent clubs of National Authorities shall also in making their domestic arrangements make such regulations as are deemed necessary to govern their club competitions, but such regulations shall comply with the Laws of the Game, and be approved by the Council of their National Authority.

68. National Visiting Teams or Sides No team or side of bowlers visiting overseas or the British Isles shall be recognised by the World Bowls Board unless it first be sanctioned and recommended by the National Authority to which its members are affiliated.

69. Contracting out No club or club management committee or any individual shall have the right or power to contract out of any of the Laws of the Game as laid down by the World Bowls Board.

REGULATING SINGLE-HANDED, PAIRS, AND TRIPLE GAMES

70. The foregoing laws, where applicable, shall also apply to Single-Handed, Pairs and Triples games.

SPECTATORS

71. Persons not engaged in the game shall be situated clear of and beyond the limits of the rink of play, and clear of the verges. They shall neither by word nor act disturb or advise the players. This shall not apply to advice given by a Manager or in his absence his delegated deputy of a team or side.

Betting or gambling in connection with any game or games shall not be permitted or engaged in within the grounds of any constituent club.

DUTIES OF MARKER

72. (a) In the absence of the Umpire, the marker shall control the game in accordance with the W.B.B. Basic Laws. He shall, before play commences, examine all bowls for the imprint of the I.B.B./W.B.B. Stamp, or that of its National

Authority, such imprint to be clearly visible, and shall ascertain by measurement the width of the rink of play (see note after Law 73).

(b) He shall centre the jack, and shall place a full length jack two yards (1.84 metres) from the ditch.

(c) He shall ensure that the jack is not less than 70 feet (21.35 metres) from the front edge of the mat, after it has been centred.

(d) He shall stand at one side of the rink, and to the rear of the jack.

(e) He shall answer affirmatively or negatively a player's inquiry as to whether a bowl is jack high. If requested, he shall indicate the distance of any bowl from the jack, or from any other bowl, and also, if requested, indicate which bowl he thinks is shot and/or the relative position of any other bowl.

(f) Subject to contrary directions from either opponent under Law 34, he shall mark all touchers immediately they come to rest, and remove chalk marks from non-touchers. With the agreement of both opponents he shall remove all dead bowls from the green and the ditch. He shall mark the positions of the jack and touchers which are in the ditch. (see Laws 33 and 40).

(g) He shall not move, or cause to be moved, either jack or bowls until each player has agreed to the number of shots.

(h) He shall measure carefully all doubtful shots when requested by either player. If unable to come to a decision satisfactory to the players, he shall call in an Umpire. If an official Umpire has not been appointed, the marker shall select one. The decision of the Umpire shall be final.

(i) He shall enter the score at each end, and shall intimate to the players the state of the game. When the game is finished, he shall see that the score card, containing the names of the players, is signed by the players, and disposed of in accordance with the rules of the competition.

DUTIES OF UMPIRE

73. An Umpire shall be appointed by the Controlling Body of the Association, Club or Tournament Management Committee. His duties shall be as follows: **(a)** He shall examine all bowls for the imprint of the I.B.B./W.B.B. Stamp, or that of its National Authority, and ascertain by measurement the width of the rinks of play. **(b)** He shall measure any shot or shots in dispute, and for this purpose shall use a suitable measure. His decision shall be final. **(c)** He shall decide all questions as to the distance of the mat from the ditch, and the jack from the mat. **(d)** He shall decide as to whether or not jack and/or bowls are in play. **(e)** He shall enforce the Laws of the Game. **(f)** In World Bowls Championships and Commonwealth Games, the umpire's decision shall be final in respect of any breach of a Law, except that, upon questions relating to the meaning or interpretation of any Law there shall be a right to appeal to the controlling body.

WORLD BOWLS BOARD BY-LAWS
PROFESSIONAL BOWLER

All players are eligible for selection for Commonwealth Games except those whose principal source of income is derived from playing the Game of Bowls.

STAMPING OF BOWLS

Each bowl complying with the requirements of Law 9 of the Board's Law shall be stamped with the official stamp of the Board. The currency of the stamp shall be for a period of 10 (ten) years expiring on 31 December and the imprint of the bowl shall record the latest year in which such bowl may be validly used.

Any Member National Authority may make its own arrangements for testing and stamping of bowls, and such bowls shall be valid for play in all matches controlled by that Authority.

Manufacturers/Testers will be entitled to use the registered I.B.B./W.B.B. stamp, to facilitate the imprint between the inner and outer rings of Bowls. Imprints on running surfaces should be avoided wherever possible.

STAMP DETAILS

B**I**B – International Bowling Board
A – Denotes code letter of Manufacturer/Tester
Numerals – Denotes year of expiry
R – Denotes that the stamp is a registered trade mark

During 1993 a new W.B.B. Stamp will be introduced and will be phased in gradually, so that by 1 January 1994 all new and retested Bowls will be stamped with the W.B.B. stamp.

The I.B.B. stamp on a Bowl will remain valid until the existing stamp expires.

METRIC EQUIVALENTS

In connection with the manufacture of Bowls there is no objection to manufacturers using metric equivalents in lieu of the present figures, always provided that Law 9 of the Board's Laws is complied with. Furthermore, there is no objection to manufacturers indicating various sizes of Bowls by numerals, and the manufacturers will be entitled to use the table on page 4 if they so desire.